First published 2008 AD
This edition © Wooden Books Ltd 2008 AD

Published by Wooden Books Ltd.
8A Market Place, Glastonbury, Somerset

British Library Cataloguing in Publication Data
Laugh
Bender Heaven

A CIP catalogue record for this book is
available from the British Library

ISBN 978 1904263 69 2

Printed and bound in England by
The Cromwell Press, Trowbridge, Wiltshire.
100% recycled papers supplied by Paperback.

BENDER
HEAVEN

written and illustrated by
Laugh

with additional drawings by Dan Goodfellow

I would like to dedicate this book to the spirit of the Dongas—the understanding that a reconnection with the land is vital for both our physical and our spiritual wellbeing; the understanding that the Earth begat us, it sustains us and it will consume us, and that our brief time in this form is both a beautiful gift to be celebrated and a huge responsibility to be born; the understanding that we are the spirit of nature personified, and that we must seek harmony and balance with our creator; the understanding that that's enough hippy bollox for one book and isn't it supposed to be about benders anyway!

We are the waking breath, we are the spirit of the earth,
we are alive and walking where we are is beautiful

Donga Alex

CONTENTS

Introduction	1
Choosing a Site	2
Siting in Winter	4
Essential Equipment	6
Poles	8
Ropes and Pegs	10
Making Pegs	12
Stressing and Setting Poles	14
Traditional Design	16
The Ridge Pole	18
The Wurzel	20
Tarps, Linings & Groundsheets	22
Dressing your Bender	24
Doors and Windows	26
Outside Fires	28
Making Fire	30
Fire Control	32
Fire Shelter	34
Cooking Outdoors	36
Woodburners	38
Woodburner Use	40
Woodburner Safety	42
General Safety	44
Environmental Impact	46
Intruders	48
Transport	50
Handcarts	52
Benders and the Future	54

All over Britain thousands of people already live in bender-type structures, some hidden in shady woodland, others down dusty tracks, many on settled sites, the rest being nomadic, building them wherever they find themselves.

INTRODUCTION

For the price of a tarpaulin and a few bits of rope anyone can create a bender. The designs are simple and the materials are relatively easy to acquire.

Be it the need for somewhere cheap to live that will cope with the elements or just the need to be closer to nature, the bender will accommodate with ease.

The origins of the bender are hard to pin down as many indigenous peoples use variations on the theme. Siberian nomads used a structure very similar to current creations using willow rods for the frames with a reindeer skin covering. Mbuti pygmies in the Congo use a bender-type frame from local wood with a covering of Mongongo leaves threaded together on lengths of string.

The bender's re-emergence in the British psyche must derive some of its influence from Kalderash gypsies arriving from Eastern Europe. Before the emergence of horse-drawn wagons several hundred years ago, these people used family-sized benders (two ridge pole benders attached to a tipi frame for stability) for everyday living, employing local wood for construction and tarpaulin for covering much the same as today.

Benders with a virtually identical design to that of the Kalderash were also introduced to English travellers in the 1970's, by Scottish tinkers who knew them as 'barrachs'.

CHOOSING A SITE
creating the space

The weather systems in northern Europe necessitate a certain amount of forethought when choosing a site for your dwelling, even in the middle of summer.

During long dry spells it is tempting to choose a site out in the open but as soon as the sun starts beating down you may wish you'd stayed in the shade. The sides of a bender can be rolled up or roped and pegged out and loosely propped up with poles to create a Bedouin tent-style affair. This will create some air circulation but as soon as the wind dies you don't want to be under a tarp in the open. Instead of moving the whole bender, you could just move the outside fire into the shade and have the best of both worlds.

As well as its obvious sanitary uses the spade is also an essential piece of safety equipment during long dry spells, as it's ideal for beating out bush fires. If enough care is not taken in the siting of an outside fire, long grasses and tall reeds as well as providing an idyllic surround for your mid-summer dreams, could also provide a perfect wick for your worst nightmare. If you've no choice but to pitch in the long grass, tear it off or cut it in a large circle round your fire pit. It may also be a wise precaution to do the same around your bender, just to be on the safe side. The same also goes for dry dead leaves or indeed any nearby combustible material which may be innocuously drying to a tinder in the sunshine.

*On a hot summer's day you can either roll up the sides of your bender
or, with a few poles, create a shady Bedouin-style affair.*

SITING IN WINTER
planning for the cold

During the other eleven and a half months of the year, wet and wind will need to be accounted for. When scanning the area you wish to pitch in, looking for that perfect flat spot under that perfect oak tree, it's always worth conjuring up a quick worst case weather scenario, just to be on the safe side.

Unless you fancy waking up in a swimming pool, you'll be looking for somewhere on higher ground, preferably with shelter to the south-west, (and north, and east as well at times).

It may be tempting to tuck right up under a safe looking tree or hedgerow for shelter in heavy weather, but if you only have a few rugs and a groundsheet between you and the earth, be sure to check for tree roots first. Also remember to check for any leaning or dead trees that may be within striking distance of your dwelling or fire circle.

Siting your doorway so you can gaze out over that beautiful valley is all very idyllic, but should a storm pick up you may find you're pointing in the wrong direction. Although in theory you can just close your door up and open a new one on the opposite side, it's usually not that simple, especially during a high wind and driving rain. If the weather has you bender bound for a few days a billowing wet door-blanket is not the sort of company you need to invite.

To avoid the worst of the weather your doorway is generally best off facing toward the south east.

The more care you take in choosing your site and positioning your bender, the more chance you have of keeping both the weather and your marbles where they belong.

5

ESSENTIAL EQUIPMENT
tools of the trade

Having the right equipment about you will always make lighter work of any task, and bender-building is no exception. First you will need a small bow saw, the triangular variety being your best bet as it gets into places other bow saws won't reach. It should have a green wood blade, the type with a circular recess every few teeth for removing the thick sawdust fibres from living wood. A bow saw with a straight saw-toothed blade may suffice, but it will probably stick a bit as it's designed for seasoned wood.

Next you will need a billhook or small axe, the sharper the better. The old hand-forged tools are usually far superior to the modern mass produced plate steel equivalents and easier to get sharp, and keep sharp. You can use an angle-grinder or a metal file to get a sharp but short lived edge, then using a whetstone (a bit of an art) you can hone it's sharpness. Make the cutting edge taper gently rather than it having 'shoulders', and it should slice through green wood pole like a knife through organic goats cheese.

The only other tools you may need for a standard woven bender are a bit of string and a knife to cut it with. Sisal or old bootlaces can provide the cordage and brands such as Taylors or Opinel can provide a decent blade.

If you are building a slot-together kit bender an auger and bit or some kind of drill may be necessary (unless you have the time and patience to use a hot iron spike). You may also find that a large G-clamp or some kind of vice will make the job a little easier.

*A bow saw, a billhook or small axe, a penknife and a few bits of string
are all the tools you need to construct a bender*

POLES
selecting and sharpening

As much of the UK is rich in fast growing softwoods, bender poles will usually be found in the vicinity of your bender site. However, if you do have to go exploring over a few miles, a large hedgerow or small woodland is your best bet.

The woods of choice are hazel and willow, which often grow in thick clumps of upright poles and have fibres that are less likely to break under pressure, but most woods will be usable as some stage in their development.

A clump or stand is best when its light has been shaded by other stands or trees so the poles reach up to the light making a gentle taper over the whole length.

Having selected the longest straightest poles of a 1 – 1½ inch diameter at the butt end, cut them as close to the ground as possible to prevent re-growth from the stump. This will provide you with a better crop of poles next time and also look a lot more pleasant to the eye.

Where possible, try to slope your cut outwards as well, so rain doesn't run into the centre of the stand, as this may eventually lead to its premature demise.

To sharpen poles, find a tree stump or large branch to use as a chopping block. Try to make long tapering cuts, and rather than cutting it down to a spike leave the tip flat, as this will prevent it splaying out if it meets a stone later when being driven into the ground.

Ropes and Pegs
installing the bender

Good ropes are important and come in different forms: Traditional hemp rope may be available through an army surplus dealer, climbing rope is expensive and only available through a specialist, and you can find nylon rope in most DIY stores.

In the colder months a rope around the outside of the bender 8-10 inches from the ground is essential. It should hold the rolled bottom edge of the tarp down, and pull it tight in against the poles, keeping out the wind and weather. When tying the ends of this rope it is best to use a peg either side of the doorway to secure it, as tying any rope under tension to your frame may pull it out of shape. You may also need to secure it to the ground with another short length and peg in one or two places round the outside edge to stop it riding up.

As soon as heavy wind occurs you'll be glad you put a few ropes over the top as well. Doing this in the dark and the rain, on a windy hilltop, although exhilarating, is not an experience you need to have. With a few well-placed ropes, good pegging and a reasonably sturdy design, a bender in 90 mph winds on open ground will survive the night intact. Not a claim you can attach to many shop-bought alternatives.

If you use eyelets sewn on to the outside of the tarp as an alternative to roping over the top, bear in mind that over time this will stretch the tarp out of shape and open the weave to the elements in places.

As well as a rope around the base, a few ropes over the top will be necessary to prevent high winds removing your tarp.

Making Pegs
woodworking for stability

You can make blanks for your pegs from either splitting a 2-3 inch diameter log in two, or a 5-8 inch diameter log into 6 or 8 pieces. Pegs should be at least 10 inches long and even longer for pitching on soft ground. A lateral cut must be made with a bow saw, a quarter to a third of the way through each blank on the long edge, about a fifth to a quarter of the way down it.

Next you will need a billhook or small axe and a chopping block. Put a long point with sweeping cuts into the end furthest from the rope slot, as with the pole-ends earlier trying to leave a small flat spot at the tip to prevent it splaying out if it comes into contact with a stone when being driven into the ground, a flat tip being more likely to push the stone aside.

To make the rope slot hold the point uppermost, cutting down from an inch or two above the lateral saw cut. Slice into the wood at an angle (less than 45 degrees), cutting a triangle shape out of the wood.

Next, holding the peg in the same position, cut a triangle the same size off the bottom of the peg, on the edge below the rope slot. This will prevent the edge above the rope slot from breaking off when the peg is struck with a mallet. You can also chamfer the blunt end with a sharp knife, taking the corners off so that when struck with a hammer the top does not flay out, rendering the peg unfit for reuse.

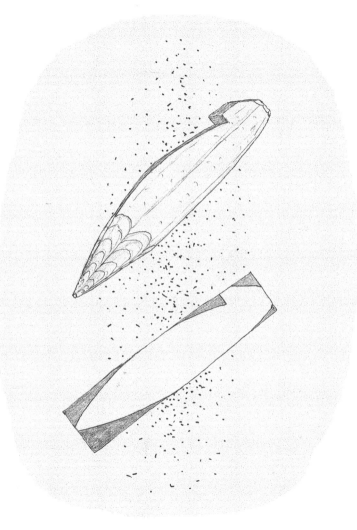

STRESSING AND SETTING POLES
tricks of the trade

The majority of poles will naturally bend further from the butt end than desired, so if the poles are not stressed or set they will try to revert back to a shape that is more comfortable to them. This can occur in 10 minutes or over a few weeks, turning your beautiful bender into a narrow, arching cathedral. Using unset poles with a slot-together bender design can split a ridge pole *(pages 18-19)* down its length and even put the toughest of wurzels *(pages 20-21)* to the test.

To stress poles, start about 2 ft up the pole from the butt end, place your hands a foot or more apart, then pull the pole against your knee or push it against a tree. Bend the pole until you hear the fibres along the far edge starting to part, move up the pole several times at 8 inch intervals, repeating the process. Then go back over it all one more time.

After stressing it's always worth staking your poles out for a few weeks to set them into shape to prevent them returning to type. 2-3 weeks in mid-summer should be adequate whereas 4-6 weeks is preferable in mid-winter. You can use fire to accelerate the process but this may lead to brittleness and a shorter lifespan.

Prepare a number of 2 ft long stakes with a point on one end, and use these to set your poles into shape. It is usually necessary to set them in batches of 5-6 poles as any more than that will force the stakes out of the ground.

After a good stressing, stake your bender poles out to set them or alternatively string them in a bow.

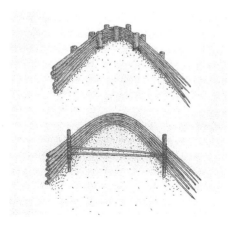

TRADITIONAL DESIGN
simple pole layout

If your poles are unset and straight from the hedgerow they will ideally first need to be stressed, the butt ends should have a point and the side branches trimmed off (unless they look like they will weave into the structure). The whole length of the pole may be useful for weaving so don't cut the top off.

When you've chosen a site imagine the bender in situ, how large it is depending on tarp size, and where the doorway is situated.

First of all, select your thickest poles and, bearing in mind where the doorway will be, position them an equal distance apart round the circumference.

If the ground is soft, drive the butt end in as far as it will go – 8 inches minimum, more for unset poles.

If the ground is hard, use a hard wood or metal stake to make a pilot hole for your poles with a 6 inch minimum depth and more again for unset poles.

Depending on your choice of wood the poles may weave together and wrap around each other easily, or you may need an amount of string to keep the poles in place. When adding more poles, the more they can be woven into the structure rather than tied, the stronger your bender is likely to become.

Don't worry if your bender seems a bit flimsy at first, each new pole adds more strength to the structure and it will not attain total stability until the tarps and ropes are in place.

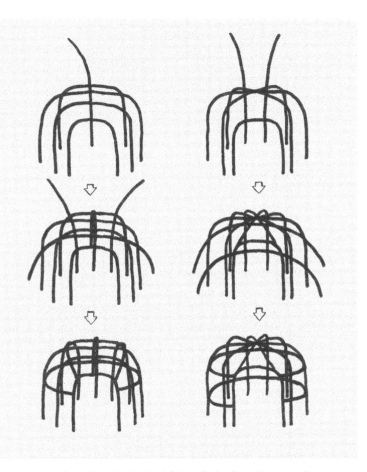

Two basic forms of bender: On the left the ridge bender, with its central spine.
On the right the centred bender, with its central gathering of poles.
Both these forms evolve on the next two pages.

THE RIDGE POLE
central balance

A ridge pole bender consists of a central pole with radiating ribs. Using a hardwood pole will vastly increase the life span of your ridge pole, though a softwood pole with set bender poles should still last for months.

Use an electric drill of an auger and bit, and a ¾ inch or 1 inch drill bit, or a length or iron rod heated to red hot in the fire if you have a few hours spare. Drill your first hole at least 4 inches from the pole end, then another parallel hole 2-4 inches in, then repeat this process at the other end checking your second two holes are parallel with the first two. Then move down the pole 1-2½ feet and repeat the process, checking the overall length of the pole to judge you hole positions. You can then use the ridge pole as it stands or, if you haven't done so before drilling, you can shave the holed edges flat with a billhook or drawknife, square it and round off the ends.

The poles need to be carefully selected and set, once trimmed, the tip ends may need a few slivers taking off with a good knife to make them fit the holes. Ideally the poles should slide through the hole an inch or two before it stops.

For the ends of the bender use normal bender poles and weave in or tie on as normal. Horizontal wooden poles can then be woven or tied on for strength and to stop the tarp sagging in. Alternatively you could employ the services of a half-wurzel (*next page*) attached to the end of your ridge pole.

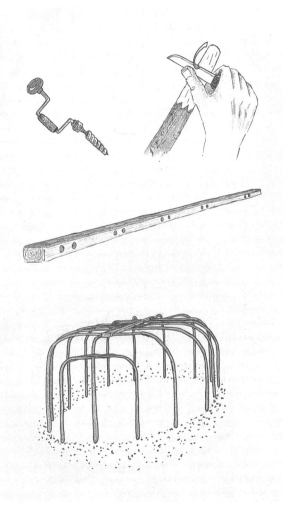

THE WURZEL
at the centre

The wurzel is so named because Romany gypsies used mangle-wurzels or turnips as a centrepiece for temporary dwellings, but if you fancy something more durable, a 4 inch deep, 10 inch diameter slice of oak or other hardwood is your best bet. You may need some form of vice to hold it, as well as a means of obtaining a slice of tree trunk and a drill.

Decide how many poles you want to go into your wurzel and mark their positions out evenly. Then, using a ¾ or 1 inch drill bit, drill the holes 2-3 inches deep around the circumference of the wurzel. Trim the pole ends to fit tightly into the holes as with the ridge pole bender.

You may require the use of a vice or a couple of G-clamps to secure the wurzel when drilling, as you want to get the drill holes square and straight, or your bender will not assume the desired shape and structural strength.

A wurzel or half-wurzel can be used in conjunction with the ridge pole bender, just trim the end of the ridge pole to slot into the wurzel adding string if necessary to keep it attached. You can also use a large wurzel for the centre of the structure and a small one for the door frame connected by a rod.

Wurzels can also be constructed from recycled or shop bought sawn timber, or a heavy duty version can be made from metal tubing and plate steel.

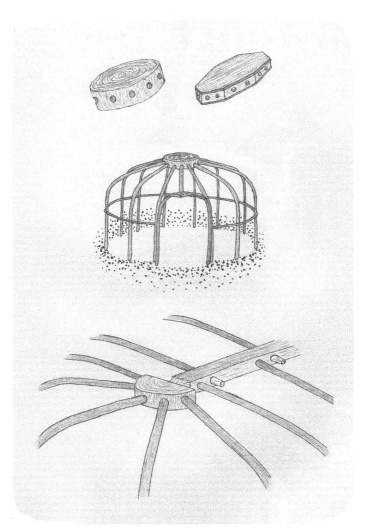

TARPS, LININGS & GROUNDSHEETS
outer and inner

If you want to get the best equipment for outdoor living, look no further than the military—a good army surplus store will be able to get hold of most of what you need. Failing that a tent or marquee manufacturer will suffice.

Heavy hemp tarpaulin is the best for insulation and water-tightness. A cotton rip-stop tarpaulin which has a nylon meshing woven in is the next choice. Ordinary cotton tarp is useable, whilst plastic lorry tarps, although convenient in a tight spot, will not breathe, instead creating condensation.

New marquee tarps, often the cheapest option, will leak like a tea-bag when the weave has been stretched and all the sealant has been washed out. Liquid sealant can be obtained from camping shops or marquee manufacturers, but once your weave is stretched the best option is a new tarp.

The best type of groundsheet is the galvanised rubber variety, being both flexible and durable. Otherwise, any type of plastic or waterproof material will do. Also it is worth trying to acquire your groundsheet in one whole piece as two or three overlapping sheets of plastic will only do the job until it rains.

As soon as the nights get chilly a lining for the inside of your bender is worth considering. Blankets and throws can provide a good insulating layer as well as a bit of colour during those dull winter evenings, or if you need a lightweight option a small cargo parachute, if obtainable, is ideal.

DRESSING YOUR BENDER
covering and lining the inside

Your bender frame will usually be a little wobbly until the tarps and ropes are in place, so it's worth taking a bit of care putting the tarp on to prevent the frame from twisting out of shape. Rather than dragging it over, it's often better to get inside and push it over bit by bit. If your bender is too tall for this you can use a flat-ended stick to hoik it over.

Your tarp should have an overlap of at least 8 inches all the way round the bottom edge of the bender. This can be rolled up from the inside to provide a tidy finish, with minimal tarp to ground contact to prevent rot.

If you don't have one whole tarp, two or three separate pieces may do the job, but they will have to be roped on well if you want them to keep the weather out. Making a skirt with the smaller pieces then putting the biggest one over the top is worth the sacrilege of cutting a few bits of tarp into lengths.

The groundsheet should also preferably have an overlap of at least 8 inches which can be folded along with the corners, back under itself. Leave a little extra on the groundsheet when folding it, so it rests up against the poles and sits off the ground to keep out the elements.

Linings are best put up once the tarp is in place. Bunch them into a length then slide them up between the poles and the tarp into the desired position before carefully opening them out. Wrap them around the poles, or tie them, to secure them into position.

A cosy, low-impact eco-home guaranteed to annoy your local planning office

DOORS AND WINDOWS
entry and exit

The simplest form of free-standing doorway is a hoop made from two medium-sized poles woven together at the top with both butt ends planted in the ground. You can choose a pole from your bender as a central door pole, attaching the highest point of the hoop to it and pushing the butt ends into the ground either side of it. Otherwise try placing the hoop next to the frame so there is no central door-pole, using one or more horizontal poles to connect it to the frame. For this type of right-angle joint string may be needed, and for that professional touch you could also use a 3 hole wurzel for the top-most joint (*see page 21*). The tarp can then be wrapped around the door hoop from the inside and a blanket secured into place to keep out the elements.

A simple porch can be created by making another hoop however many feet out from the doorway, then extending the horizontals to meet it. Attach the tarp to this doorway instead and add a second door blanket or strip of tarp. In weathery situations you will also need an extra rope over the top to pull the tarp tight over the inside door hoop to keep out draughts.

If you need a little light in your life most tent or canvas manufacturers will stitch in a clear flexible plastic window to your specifications for a price (financial and environmental), or, if there's one lying around, a conventional framed glass window can be fitted at ground level with a bit of ingenuity and imagination.

*When built with a bit of care and attention a bender can be
a surprisingly light, warm, dry, cosy and spacious home.*

OUTSIDE FIRES
and the essential kettle

When choosing the site for an outside fire always think safety first. Make sure combustibles (twigs, moss, leaves etc) are removed from within 4-6 foot or more, depending on the location. Ideally there should be bare earth beneath your fire, but lighting it on short grass is safe enough. Otherwise remove the turf with a spade. Long grasses, reeds, dead leaves and low cover such as hanging branches are the main things to look out for. It's best to be on the safe side—having to put out a bush fire that you have inadvertently started yourself is an experience worth avoiding.

Extra care is needed in the vicinity of pine needles, especially as you're also more likely to be using pine logs which create sparks when burnt. Fire can also travel underneath a bed of pine needles so if you are near pine trees make sure your fire is sited on bare earth, or better still, outside of a pine wood altogether.

The distance your outside fire needs to be from your dwelling depends on it's visibility from within. Many travelling gypsies and itinerants past used a small round bender without an internal woodburner, instead having a large open doorway with an open fire within 2-3 feet of the entrance. This is fine because you can keep constant vigil over your fire from your doorway, not forgetting to make it safe before you go to sleep or leave the site.

For firewood, avoid Elder (which does not burn) and choose dead dry wood where available. Dry out wet logs by arranging them around the fire, though keeping a watchful eye on them.

A previously unmentioned item of essential equipment is your trusty kettle.
When leaving camp always kick the embers of your fire apart
to prevent it flaring up if it gets windy while you're out.

MAKING FIRE
the ancient art of survival

To start your fire you will need some form of tinder, and some-thing to light it with. If your name is Ray Mears, you could use some Old Man's Beard (Clematis seed heads), dried moss (where it's not scarce) or dried gorse tips, along with a flint sparker. If, however, you don't mind a bit of techno, a few scrunched up bits of newspaper or even a fire-lighter will suffice, as well as that marvel of the modern world—a cheap lighter.

Secondly you will need a few handfuls of fine twigs and small sticks no more than a centimetre in diameter. These can be obtained in a nearby wooded area or hedgerow. Small dead twigs should just snap off in your hand, if you can bend them to 90° then they're probably still alive.

Kindling can also be obtained by splitting down a short log into thin sticks with a sharp axe, using a penknife to make shavings if finer kindling is needed.

For the fire's main fuel you should ideally have a selection of wood, sticks of an inch diameter all the way up to 8 inch logs would be ideal. If you only have logs then splitting a few down into smaller sections is always better than waiting an hour for the heat to build up before your big logs stop smoking and start to burn.

It's also worth remembering that fire uses oxygen as well as wood for fuel, so a loosely stacked fire will generally burn faster, and on a windy day you can stack your fire a little tighter to reduce the oxygen flow and make it last.

The same stands which may have provided your bender poles often contain dead dry lengths which make perfect firewood and can be collected at the same time.

FIRE CONTROL
outdoor safety

If your fire is sluggish and lacking draw, a little artificial wind can be created. Use a biscuit tin lid to flap the base of the fire or use a copper pipe to blow (never suck) into the embers.

To shut a fire down for the night, or if you're leaving camp for an amount of time, pull the burning logs out and lay them around the outside of your ash circle so they touch neither each other nor the embers in the centre, then spread the embers so that they are also separated. If logs are still connected to the central embers a little wind can turn them back into a roaring fire in the blink of an eye.

The wind can also create other problems regarding outside fires. You may have been wise to put the fire 6 ft away from a hedgerow or tree as protection from possible storms, but an obstruction to the wind can create eddies and pockets of swirling air, and in the case of a fire, swirling smoke can rapidly turn a potentially pleasant blustery evening under the moon into a night indoors.

If it rains in the night, unless you've got a metal dustbin lid on legs or similar ingenious device, you'll wake up to a soggy pit of ashes. Re-lighting a fire in these conditions can cause problems. However, if the ground is not too saturated a layer of lateral sticks or a few sheets of newspaper should provide enough of a dry base to rebuild your fire on.

Fire is one of the best ways of advertising your presence—to avoid smoke, make a small hot fire from only the driest wood.

*Whether indoors or outdoors, keep flammable objects at a safe distance
from fire, and fire will continue to be your friend.*

FIRE SHELTER
protection from the elements

Another tried and tested method of keeping the rain off your fire is the fire shelter. With an extra tarpaulin, a few bits of rope and a few sticks, the world again is your oyster. Unless you have rip-stop, make sure your tarp is an old one, as stringing it out between trees will quickly loosen the weave, turning your waterproof covering into a 'tea-bag' in no time at all.

Tilting your tarp into the wind will provide shelter, but a flow through of air is necessary to prevent the smoke from pooling. Again, if you use a central pole it's best not to have the pitch too high or you'll end up with a kipper factory. The height of your kitchen shelter depends not only on the passage of smoke but the size of your fire for obvious reasons.

If you use poles for the centre or edges of a shelter of this type it's always worth burying the base of the pole 6 inches or more into the ground especially if it's not secured at the top, otherwise the wind will at some point puff the tarp out and your falling pole will invariably boff someone on the head.

With poles used as props in this manner, an old T-shirt can be wrapped around the top and tied on, to prevent the pole damaging your tarp if a wind picks up.

Finally, it's best to avoid the temptation to attach one corner of your fire shelter to your free standing bender as it's not designed to take that sort of strain and more likely than not it will slowly change shape to compensate.

Use available tying points and a few stout poles to suspend your fire shelter, judging the height by the size of your intended fire.

COOKING OUTDOORS
back to the old ways

Cooking on an outside fire is a culinary experience all of its own. You'll need a stout pair of knees or some sort of low furniture and, unless you're happy with your pot of stew occasionally rolling off the logs and depositing its contents into the ashes, you'll need some form of iron mongery.

Most blacksmiths will know how to make a trivet. The traditional design consists of 3 or 6 horseshoes welded together into a flat pan base with 3 legs, 8 inches or more in length.

A traditional gypsy fire would see an iron tripod with a chain and hook, all the pans and kettles having appropriate handles, the advantages of this design being the ability to adjust the height of your vessel from the flames.

If you're not fussy, a traditional hippie bodge is a couple of bricks and an oven grill, barbecue style.

When you've secured your cooking pot above the flames use small sticks to bring it to the boil and gradually feed in larger logs for the constant heat needed to keep it bubbling.

The majority of your kitchen items are best kept off the ground or in a metal container if you're stopped for any length of time, as any hint of food will soon attract rodents.

Some form of rack or even an old hammock may prove useful for short term food and utensil storage. As for metal containers, army surplus ammunition boxes, if rain proof, are ideal.

Various ingenious devices can be obtained to suspend your cooking vessels above the flames of an open fire.

WOODBURNERS
gas bottles and other ideas

Woodburners come in all shapes and forms from a small home-made gas bottle burner carefully drilled, hacksawed and bolted, to a state of the art shop-bought affair. You can even visit a local blacksmith and have one made to specifications.

If attempting a gas bottle burner it should be filled with water and boiled out to avoid unnecessary explosions. Apart from that all burners follow the same basic principles.

The draw of the unit is the most important aspect. As well as a large enough door to load logs, the burner should have another opening either on or below the door. This opening regulates the air flow (or draw) and should be able to close to nothing to allow your oak log to stay in overnight, as well as being able to open wide enough to allow the fire to roar and the kettle to boil.

The burner should also have some form of metal plate or baffle to obstruct the flow of hot air from fire to flue pipe.

Although not a necessity, some form of grate can be used to allow air beneath the fire as well, providing maximum draw. If you haven't got one a few prods with a poker may suffice.

Gaps around the edges of doors or air inlets may increase your draw but they will prevent a log staying in overnight. With a good air-tight burner you should be able to open it up in the morning, pop a bit of kindling onto the embers and hop back into bed for ten minutes, while the kettle boils and the morning chill recedes.

*Lightweight burners can be made from gas bottles or even fire
extinguishers but a heavier iron burner will keep you warmer for
longer, and is more likely to stay in overnight.*

WOODBURNER USE
getting the right design

Not being able to shut your burner down properly can be dangerous should you ever need to do so in a hurry, for instance when high winds create an over-draw making the flue pipe glow red, or when you've unwittingly put on one too many pine logs, having much the same effect.

A flat top on your burner is nigh on essential if you want to cook to any degree. The aga has a circular opening on top into which fit concentric iron rings providing an adjustable diameter for transferring heat directly to any size pan. Although I'm sure someone has an aga in their bender mansion the rest of us may benefit from the technology. A metal plate and corresponding opening or hinged flip-top lid may halve the boiling time of your kettle, saving firewood in the process.

For kindling, hazel wood twigs and small sticks are ideal. A split log chopped into kindling from a softish wood like pine or ash would be a suitable alternative.

As well as kindling you need fuel to feed your burner. A good mixture of logs small enough to wrap your hand round, large logs and longer split logs is ideal.

If the wood is green (still alive) it will produce more smoke than flames. The best wood has been dead for a year and left standing so that the air can circulate round it. Firewood which is too rotten gives the same effect as green wood.

The woodburner is a hungry and fickle beast, feed it with good quality fuel and it will be your best friend, use rotten wood or green wood at your peril.

WOODBURNER SAFETY
distance, flue pipes and plates

The burner must be a safe distance from both tarp and groundsheet. Either fold the groundsheet back leaving a bare patch or use something like a paving slab as a base. A large metal plate with a lip is ideal for catching the embers that can fall out when opening your burner door.

Make sure the tarp is roped well away from the back of the burner and remember to check occasionally to see how hot it's getting back there. It's also worth a check around the outside of your bender after a windy night to make sure any ropes over the top haven't been dislodged, coming to rest on your flue.

The place where the flue exits the tarp is critical, a bodge job with wads of chicken wire will need constant attention as well as letting in the elements. Instead, a flue plate made from thin soft metal plate can easily be constructed with a few tools, or you could draw a plan and see what your local blacksmith or small engineering firm would charge.

The plate should have a hole to fit your flue pipe in the centre and drilled holes around the edge so it can be bolted to another identical plate or screwed through the tarp into strips of baton wood. The section of tarp on the inside of the screws or bolts can then be removed. The flue pipe can go vertically through the roof, or with angle sections of flexi-flue, out through the side wall, where it may need a post or stake to be wired to for stability.

A stout stick and a bit of copper wire can prevent your flue pipe creaking around on a windy night. Notice too this bender's useful porch (see page 26).

SAFETY
fire and disease precautions

The best way to view a bender in terms of safety is as a wick waiting to be lit. Fire will be your best friend, but unless kept in its place could also be your worst enemy. Candles, if used, should have proper metal holders with nothing combustible anywhere near them and should never be left unattended. If your candle holder has a drip tray make sure it is kept free from anything that could be turned into a secondary wick by a rogue candle.

Never fall asleep with a candle still burning! Using a candle as your primary light source requires a constant level of vigilance. You cannot afford to be complacent.

The main danger points to remember are any combustibles in close proximity to burner or candles, embers falling from the burner door, overdraw making the flue pipe and back of the burner glow red, and your outside fire.

It may also be worth carrying a first aid kit with disinfectants such as thyme or tea tree oil as well as bandaging for cuts etc.

Take normal hygiene precautions when cooking as well as making sure food waste is either hung in a tree or buried in a hole to avoid attracting potential disease-carrying scavengers.

Also, when walking your spade in the morning make sure you dig deep enough and cover well enough so Mr. Foxy doesn't get a free supper before he wanders into your camp at night to lick the dinner plates.

Always be vigilant with fire. Attend to candles, watch your burner,
candles and outside fire, and use your imagination and common sense to
keep yourself and those around you safe.

ENVIRONMENTAL IMPACT
landscape awareness

Though the environmental impact of a few benders dwellers for a few weeks or months is usually insignificant, it's always worth bearing your footprint in mind when choosing a site.

If you're on a designated area of natural beauty or a site of special scientific interest or an area that seems particularly unique or diverse, you will need to cast a little more of a careful eye before pitching up.

The longer you stay in one place the more your environmental impact will have to be managed, multiplied by the number of people and benders involved.

Large, long-lived encampments on sensitive sites should be avoided, especially over the winter months when environmental impact will become more acute with the additional need for firewood and the increased erosion of landscape due to human traffic over damp ground.

Totally stripping an area of dead wood will have an adverse environmental impact, decimating the insect population, which in turn provides food for birds, bats and the like, so start travelling further afield before it starts to become scarce.

When on one site for longer periods, cooked food waste and human waste may also need to be managed. A pit is the quick and easy option, as long as you dig deep and leave it covered (when not in use) to keep out four-legged trouble makers. Fill it in and dig a new one every week or so, weather depending.

The more people that come to visit you in Shangri-La, and the more guest-benders and fellow bender-dwellers join you, the more environmental impact you will be having.

INTRUDERS
rodents, badgers and bees

Rodents are everywhere so it's always worth investigating your bender pitch first rather than noticing the mouse hole under your bed from the scratching and rustling beneath your groundsheet on your first night.

Generally speaking it usually takes a while for a new bender to attract much rodent attention. Start to leave things out that they find interesting, however, and they'll come back for more ... every night, and more than likely with their extended family in tow. A metal food-box and lack of crumbs should prevent limit this kind of attention.

It's also worth keeping an eye open for ants nests or wasps nests when choosing your bender and fire sites. Badger sets are also something to keep a respectable distance from, especially if you have dogs. However quaint they may appear at first, badgers can be grumpy and noisy, they keep unsociable hours, and they may not appreciate you camping in their garden.

You are also likely to find you have attracted wasps and hornets when dismantling your bender, the folds of a tarp being an ideal place for their hibernation, as well as an ideal place for wild bees to start a little factory during the summer months.

Other unmentionable scuttlers and slitherers may arrive seeking refuge from the autumn rains. Keeping your bender hot and bone dry, however, should reduce the moisture content enough to keep most of them at bay.

Some of the local wildlife will welcome your presence, especially if you are likely to provide them with a free lunch. Other neighbours may not appreciate your presence so much

TRANSPORT
alternatives to automobiles

If you intend travelling with a bender there are a number of possibilities. The obvious option of a motor vehicle, however, can seriously limit your available choice of sites. That beautiful wooded glade or windy hilltop may be out of reach if hard standing is one of your main requirements.

The other option is some form of animal-drawn vehicle. Horses and donkeys, as well as being able to transport full covered wagons, can also pull a flat cart complete with full bender kit. This will allow you much more access to the countryside but will also provide you with a whole new kettle of fish. If you intend to be horse- or donkey-drawn it is a sensible option to consult reading matter and people with personal experience first, rather than learn at the expense of your new found friend, or the party of nuns who happen to be crossing the road in front of you as your lack of experience in handling large and dangerous animals comes to the fore.

The most self-sufficient form of animal-drawn vehicle is the handcart, and its most simple model involves the use of just one human being, namely yourself. Itinerant tradesmen or 'hedge mumpers' of days gone by used handcarts or barrows to travel the country, doing seasonal agricultural work or peddling their wares as they did their rounds.

This technology has been re-invented for the modern age with both traditional and radical designs.

The bender is ideally suited to life on the open road and is easily transported around by means of a hand-cart. However, if a horse-drawn cart is your vehicle of choice, get some experienced advice before you embark (picture by Tipi Jean).

HANDCARTS
the frugal side of benders

For a minimalist handcart you will need wood from the hedgerow, 4 x 5 inch sections of angle iron, and a handful of large wood screws or bolts. You will also need the use of your trusty bow saw, a small hacksaw and a drill to make pilot holes for bolts or screws to prevent splitting, as well as a screwdriver or spanners. Mountain bike, BMX, or small moped wheels fit beautifully into this type of design. Shafts or handles can be attached straight onto the framework for maximum strength and minimal weight, or uprights can be added to the front of the frame to jack the shafts up, leaving the bed of the handcart horizontal when in motion.

You can also get your local blacksmith to construct the basic chassis out of box section steel, attaching wheels, wooden shafts and wooden sides yourself.

The more traditionally designed handcarts usually use an axle to connect the wheels, sometimes even with leaf springs for suspension. The shafts are not in line with the wheel axles but are horizontal when the cart is in motion.

Pulling-weight and human ingenuity are your only design limitations. Your cart could be fully enclosed with drawers and compartments, beautiful wood scrolling and the paintwork of a traditional Gypsy wagon.

Handcarts have even been known to double as stages for puppet theatres and to carry slide out beds with covered wagon tops. The possibilities are endless.

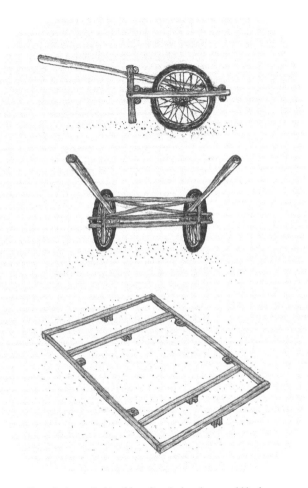

If you don't mind a bit of frugality the handcart could be for you.

BENDERS AND THE FUTURE
low cost and low impact

With the recent acquisition of knowledge about the Earth's climate and our effects upon it, environmental concerns are now becoming more widespread. An increased awareness of nature brings a realisation of the extent to which our society has become disassociated from its natural environment.

Although ultra-low-impact lifestyles cannot provide all the answers, many believe they can make the difference and should be actively encouraged as a viable option.

Thousands of people already live in bender-type structures in Britain, hidden in shady woodland or down dusty tracks, either on settled sites or following the nomadic tradition, but this type of close to nature lifestyle could accommodate many more without having an adverse effect on the land.

Bender dwelling brings an appreciation of the elements and the cycles of nature which are sadly lacking in our culture, a probable cause of our collective disregard for environmental concerns. Bender dwelling also re-introduces us to the hands-on primal skills which our ancestors needed for everyday life, and which have been the basis of human learning for hundreds of thousands of years.

If you want to find out more about bender lifestyles in Britain you can now buy various low impact publications (like this one), visit green festivals and fairs, or just take a stroll through that shady woodland or down that dusty track, and see what you can find.

POSTSCRIPT
looking at benders in a new way

I would like to thank the author of a book called *Tipi Living* for providing part of the inspiration for my spending more than ten years living with the land. I of course opted for a bender instead, but the basic principal is the same.

Like he, I have also felt the urge to pass on some of the experience and insight I have gained, in the desire to let others know of possibilities they may not have considered.

For myself, the bender's beauty is its ability to provide a simple, cheap, low impact, self-build shelter that can be substantial and comfortable enough to live in all year round.

The added bonus of providing the opportunity to live face to face with our environment whilst still maintaining a few of the comforts and conveniences of modern life, is something to be treasured. A thunderstorm when viewed from your bender doorway is like no other, and to be woken by birdsong, and watch the sun rise to the boiling of a kettle on an open fire is always a profound experience.

If nothing else it goes to show that we don't have to be slaves to conventionality. If convention doesn't suit or fails to provide what we need, we can make our own way, explore different lifestyles and even create new ways of living if we so wish ... the choice is ours.

Happy hedge mumping!!!

The lowest-cost, lowest impact, most sustainable dwelling possible.